T0128721

Freedom in the

Power

of the

Pen

Paulette Hunt Montgomery
Edited by Tracy Arnold
and
Jessica Boyd

authorHOUSE®

AuthorHouse™
1663 Liberty Drive
Bloomington, IN 47403
www.authorhouse.com
Phone: 1 (800) 839-8640

Published by AuthorHouse 05/27/2016

ISBN: 978-1-5246-0432-5 (sc)
ISBN: 978-1-5246-0433-2 (hc)
ISBN: 978-1-5246-0431-8 (e)

Library of Congress Control Number: 2016906344

Print information available on the last page.

This book is printed on acid-free paper.

Dedication

I dedicate this book to the best poet I know,
my mother Barbara Ruth Smith Hunt.
To my husband, Ricardo whose love, understanding
and unconditional support is my daily inspiration
and I thank God for blessing me with you.
My mentor and friend, Betty Knight and Felicia LecQue.

Acknowledgments

First and foremost, I thank God for giving me the courage to write this book and for placing people around me who believe in me.

To my daughter and son, Zoie and Carlos Montgomery; you are my greatest gifts. I love you guys endlessly, and I thank God for blessing me with you. As you get older, just know that "Freedom is always in the Power of the Pen." Don't be afraid to speak up and at times, speak out. Always remember to keep God, first and that all things are possible.

To my sister Terri Hunt, you have been a great role model and friend. I thank and love you for your unconditional support and love, especially during "those days." I find strength in all that you do. I am the woman that I am, because you have sacrificed so much for me and your other siblings. I am proud to be your sister and friend.

Special thanks to my brothers and sister Darryl, Paul and Shawnee Hunt, my mother and sister-in-law Janet Montgomery and Sophia Arrington, along with my extended family in the military for your love and support. A warm, heartfelt thanks to my sisters that were in Afghanistan with me.

Last but certainly not least, thank you to my ninth grade teacher, Ms. Mary Buttell, for saving me when my voice had fallen upon deaf ears. I thank you for hearing my cry and having the courage to make a change and a long lasting impression on a young girl's life.

In Loving Memory of
My father and brother, Robert Lee Hunt Sr. and Jr.

Table of Contents

A Time

History is important to me, and it's a shame that they don't teach black history in elementary school: like Otis Boykin, Dorothy Height, or Dr. Daniel Hale Williams. Because some people think that black folks have not made a proper contribution to this country, it's funny to me, because we were the last of God's people to be set free. "Certain" books were not allowed through the doors of public schools for colored people to see and it's still the same in the 21st century.

Slavery was abolished when, *yeah,* in 1865, and I thank Pennsylvania for being the first state to let my people go, and years down the line other states relinquished the power and let them flee. Sadly, Texas was the last to give up their authority.

Now take a journey with me, when time defines the line, when cruelty and injustice affected only black mankind. A time when a mother muffled the sound of a sick child, to avoid the heat of the men riding horses in white sheets. Crosses lit the Jamestown streets. A time when colored folks were afraid to speak, for fear of getting beat.

Even though, I walk through the valley of death, I will fear no evil. **I am** made in the image of God with wool like hair and **THIS** is not a sequel! So my people, it is time to **wake up**, **get up** and be on your way because your ancestor worked too hard for you to keep your **butt** in bed today.

This is not a time for you to go astray, but a moment of silence as we reflect on the pain, sorrow, and suffering of yesterday. Nooowww, some folks don't want to look back because they are embarrassed and ashamed that their ancestors could have done, all that!

All "what" you say, take Kings and Queens from their native land, take a crying baby from her mother's hands, look at the teeth and gums of a free man, glance him over once and say "**you will work my land.**" Took the King's prize and used her for a belly warmer. Knowing that if the colored man would have glanced at Miss Millie from any direction, you would have stripped him down, beat him twice, hung him from the nearest tree as his wife and children watched, idly.

As they looked to the sky asking, "Why?" with water streaming freely from their eyes. "Lord, what did we do to deserve such unrighteousness?" "I knooowww you feel my pain. **Please**, keep my mental capacity together, so I don't go insane?"

As they embraced one another, they remained strong, as they humbled themselves and sang old Negro spiritual songs, "We shall overcome one day, for I know in my heart. Yes, I do believe we shall overcome."

After 246 years of misery, 40 million died and paved the way for me and now my people of color don't have to shed unnecessary tears of fears brought on at night because their skin tone "isn't" light.

All this came to be, because you couldn't see that you looked like me. You judged me not for me, but because the color of my skin made you feel uneasy, and the fear in you're their heart made you hate me and your subconscious mind could not let me be free.

Now I'm happy as hell that time did prevail, because liberty and justice wasn't for someone who looks like me. And I reckon, as my grandmother would say, the more things change, they stay the same; because on June 7, 1998, a black man was drug by chains and all, **ALL** of America should have stood up and said **that's** a damn shame.

Take your foolish pride, set it aside, and realize that prejudice, and hatred make you die inside. Open your eyes, so you can see, that we are no longer slaves to a country that once rejected thee. There is no need to flee because your ancestor knew this day would come to be.

Now stand with pride and wipe the tears away from yesterday; and look at your neighbor and say, "**NEIGHBOR**, we can and will make it through better days. Life is a test of time and it is by God's great design that, you and I are here; enjoy the sunshine and fresh air. Now don't be fooled, for there are rules for us to obey and you will find out if you pass the test on judgment day."

Back From War

Back from the war, three times I've stored things deep within my cranium walls. It's like an overstuffed closet, trying to shut the door before things fall. I can't get a grip. My words are not always pleasant that come from my lips. I'm home and yet I'm alone as the walls close in on me. I suddenly feel claustrophobic and I can't breathe. My family and friends say that I have changed. I hear the sounds of bullets flying around as mortars hit the ground from all sides. Siren sounds startle me. The forces of nature cause me to get down as I let out a familiar sound "In Coming" with my face buried in the ground.

Images from the war quest my dreams, waking up in a cold sweats causes me to pace the floor, scanning my sector from windows to doors. Afraid to drift back to sleep because the boogieman is chasing me, I'm uptight; something's not right, my mind is at a double time, day and night. I have to shake the cobwebs out and make sure my uniform is right, because at the Brigade level you aren't shit if you can't go and fight.

My truthfulness on questionnaires at sick call leads to a personal escort down the hall, and I will admit I was nervous as hell because the soldiers had me surrounded as if I had just broken out of jail. Looking in the mirror, I see that I have changed. Crying and I don't know why my body hurts from all sides. I'm frustrated because I can't remember what happened yesterday, but I can give you in detail, what happened five years ago as if it were today.

Now my days and weeks are filled with multiple appointments, as I try to figure out how to decompress and drop this heavy load, so my mind doesn't explode. "I look around the room and let the lady know that I can't stay, I have to go." You don't understand that if word gets out, from time to time, I have to rest on the couch. You might as well say my career is over and lights out. Nothing is confidential, as they say. I can see myself walking up to formation and the whisper of the crazy/coo-coo is coming our way.

Uncle Sam, I'm talking to you today. I gave you the best of me, dedicated to the cause so others could rest in peace. Made sacrifices for the Red, White and Blue because that is what real patriots do. Nine eleven, (9/11) came around and the kid from Nebraska could still be found. Doing my part 24/7 non-stop for a country that I love and at birth stole my heart. Now that my ailment lay behind my frontal lobe, hidden from the human eyes, I hope that you have the fortitude to raise your right hand and not disappear with the wind. And repeat after me; "I, United States of America, do willingly promise to protect and defend you, soldier and friend from all enemies foreign and domestic, and those in disguise on the rich soil trying to hide. For you are now encompassed into the constitution for which young men and women died. I will be loyal to you as you were to this great nation night after night. I'm willing to give it all for the brave ones who kept this homeland tight. I will see that you get the best of the best to recover from all scars. Now rest with ease, knowing I am here to assist thee. For this is my pledge to you, so help me God."

Black Woman

I'm a black woman with black dreams.
Married to a black man with two black kids that look like me.
I believe in black love indeed.
My man is my King and I'm his Queen.
Humble and meek, ladylike at all times and if need to,
I will check a fool for getting out of line.

Always walking with my head held high,
For I have lost nothing on the ground,
So my eyes do not reside there.
Besides, I want to acknowledge people,
As they walk by and stare,
As my confidence spills out in my stride.

I'm not afraid of my black skin because black,
Mixed in with other colors is a beautiful revolution,
That runs deep to produce multiple shades on this earth.
Sugar Brown, Caramel Cream,
Dark Chocolate from the African seed, Red Bone,
And Yellow Tone is a reflection of who I be.

So please stare at me. I will not hide my face for I am
A bold, black, beautiful woman with style and grace.
So don't you dare call me out of my race?

For I have learned to love and embrace my identity.
A strong black woman comfortable in my own skin,
With a powerful mind for the world to see as I take center
stage.
With my wool like hair and last year's shades,
With my ancestor's features on display, with my big nose,
big lips, big ass, and big hips for these beautiful features
Some folks pay big dollars to get.

Now, how lucky am I to be a jewel,
To be seen because of the genetic makeup of my genes.
For black is beautiful and I'm claiming it.
For black I am and black is who I will be,
And I thank God for putting his paint brush on me.

Carlos

I'm full of pride; looking into my baby boy's eyes, seeing a reflection of me. Trying to look deep into his soul I wonder what the future holds and who will be the man to transpire from his frame. Some nights I creep through the hall, standing in his doorway. The shadow that cascades off the wall from his night light makes me seem tall. Knowing by the end of the summer he will pass me by as we stand side by side, the giant (his mother) all of 4 feet 10 inches tall. Watching him sleep, I thank God for blessing me with a son that means more than life to me.

Remembering the feeling and the joy of holding my baby boy for the first time, is indescribable. It opened me up internally, took in the moment that took my breath away. I sobbed uncontrollably, looked at his little fingers and toes, I smiled because he has my nose. Wondering how this picture will unfold. Hoping I have what it takes, as a woman, to raise this boy into a man. Knowing I am going to make mistakes and be on trial daily.

For a mother wears many hats. Therefore, I am the teacher, playmate, doctor, disciplinarian, taxi, judge, jury, maid, counselor, coach, referee, protector and friend. I am resilient like the force of nature, for a mother's job never ends.

So, my son, I know at times I'm hard as hell, but I'm doing the best I can to protect you from the bars that cause bail. My emotion runs high and some days I look at you and cry. Not because I'm sad, but because you're growing so fast. I want to make sure I'm giving you the right tools to survive in this corrupt world, called life.

The Lord has given you a powerful mind, so while they sleep, you have to feed your brain cells with his words and fully understand that knowledge is power and power is freedom. Freedom in the sense to be fearless, respectful, enduring, enlightening, determined, omniscient and mindful of being the man you want the world to see, and not the distorted image of who they portray you to be. Be the man who dares himself to be great; the man with the will, desire, and discipline to move heaven's gates. The man who sees in his mother's eyes the hard work and sacrifice, along with the internal drive inside to give her baby boy the best that she could.

My baby boy, it has been my joy to watch you grow to be the young man that you are now, and I long to see the man that you'll become. Remember to stay true to yourself and follow all of your dreams. Keep God first and you will always have a fresh start. Know that mama loves you with all of her heart.

Do Not Weep For Me

As your cup runneth over, do not weep for me.
I know that you have asked God "Why?"
Perhaps you have said a few things to our father that wasn't nice,
but at times like these, I'm sure he'll let you slide.
Do not weep for me, for we are destined to live and die.
I've lived a good life with a wonderful husband,
And four beautiful, daughters, and grandchildren,
Making special times as the years went by.

Do not weep for me, for I am always in your heart.
This is not the ending, but the beginning,
Of a new chapter that you must start.
Remember me healthy and strong,
Walking through the house singing my favorite song.

If I could have taken you all with me, I would have,
But that would have been selfish.
Besides, God is not finished grooming you to be,
The person that he needs and wants you to be.
Do not hide in the dark, for the darkness smothers your pain.
Find the courage to rejoice, in calling out His name.

Do not weep for me, for I am in a better place.
And I long to once again see the look upon your face.

Defend

We have been at war to explore the grounds where dragons lay to slay their people, to conform to a way of life that strips them of their human rights as they remain helpless in their land, wanting to fight back. They are afraid of the repercussions that their actions would play (sounds like a form of slavery not in the USA). Their dictatorship rules caused an uproar that influenced the Red, White and Blue to move in their direction with a firm step that would not be ignored. We dressed for the occasion to protect and defend those who could not defend themselves.

The altercation between the Israelis and Palestinians was simmering and on the rise. We fall in line to catch their tears. While we put the weight of their issues on our shoulders, ignoring our situation at home, our enemy observed our actions, knowing that we left the women and children alone. Thinking we're the great knights that had to run to everyone's rescue and fight, some countries warned us about what they would do. They shouted out, "We don't want you here, you're too busy in other country's affairs," not knowing the unforeseen moment was brewing in the air.

It's hard for me to sleep; my anxiety is taking over me and the Kuwaiti air is heavy, as I try to count sheep. I drift in rest knowing that my mission tomorrow will put me on the road counting all fingers and toes, hoping to stay alert to find all Individual Explosive Devices (IED) hidden in the road. Now I'm on my way, with sixty other soldiers hitting the pavement this day. As the time approaches us, the faces change as the stress jumps outside of the normal range. I take a deep breath and this is what I pray.

"Lord, we come to you humble and on bended knees, and in our silent, uncertain moment, please protect these brave men and women and hear our plea. As we come face to face with the enemy, guide our trucks to avoid the IEDs and hear the sound of the oppositions approaching fleet, and help me warn others following me. May our training be at its peak as we take to the Iraqi streets, hoping to make it back through the safety gate? If this is the road that I shall lay my helmet, sword, and shield down, let me suffer no more and send an angel right away." Filling my lungs for the last time, I whisper and say, "My Father who art in heaven, thank you for blessing me to see the beauty of your land and giving me a family that loves me as I am. Lord, please put them at ease and help them to remember all the wonderful memories. I was the gift that you gave to thee, for this is the last time you will hear me say, I love you Lord and forgive me of all sin, as you take my breath away."

Eyes Wide Open

Eyes wide open and yet I cannot see,
The multiple colors that surround me.
Could it be that the teardrops have my vision,
Hazy, or am I a mere illusion to the,
World and nothing phases me?

I've been walking in the dark for years.
Being alone has brought insecurity and much fears.

How do I tell the demons to flee? When I can't find,
The strength or the courage to fall to my knees, and
I often wonder if God still loves me.

Fingertips

He had me on my knees; body, soul and mind open freely,
As I allow him to bury his manhood deep, deep inside me,
Consistently pleasing me, till tears ran down my face as our
Bodies connected over and over again, there was no space
between us.

I screamed out in shame of loving a man so much,
That I am insane in the membrane, by the way he restores me.
I gave it up endlessly, turning my body like a pretzel,
Aiming to please thee.

My friends say that I'm crazy, because I walk around
With a smile on my face just thinking about yesterday.
My hands roam my anatomy and I get hot flashes,
Fantasizing about him near me, touching me, inside of me,
defining me.

His fingertips caress me like the keys on a piano.
The music we make is as complicated as Mozart,
As it leaves us breathless.

He looked deep into my eyes, buried three of his phalanges
In my sweet cherry pie and then licked them clean,

I'm so turned on that I start to scream.
"Kiss me passionately until every hole opens freely.
Make me scream your name, Make me yell in vain,
Hit this love box right as you envision me sucking "Your"
candy cane".

You're the superstar tonight Poppy,
And there is no shame in my game,
I'm better than McDonalds, I'm like BK,
And you can have it your way.

Because he aims to please and I'm mesmerized,
By the sensation of having both spots filled with ease.
Instantly, I become an addict, because I have to have it,
As he works his magic wand. He's got me balled up,
Pinned up, tears rolling down my face.
Love box and body feeling so good,
I'm somewhere floating in space.

His hands firmly grip my breast, putting my body to the test,
Pinching my nipples. That brought delightful pain,
As my love box pulsated, until I uh, uh aw.
Bringing me back one more time, as my organism builds to
its peak.
I am humping, and grinding like a super freak,

As we climax together our bodies fall limp on the damp sheets.

His fingertips caress me like the keys on the piano,
As my consciousness starts to fade,
I think to myself how can I make tomorrow better than today.

First To Fight

First to fight for the rights and to build our nation's might;
Dr. Martin Luther King did it resiliently night after night,
So that every man, woman, boy, and girl could have equality
And the same rights.

Everyone needs to possess these qualities that come from within
As he did and realize that his tenacity was his best friend.
A man with a dream, not a scheme, stood on a mountain
Top so he could hear the bells ring.
As the sky opened wide, our father embraced him by his side,
And said for the journey you take my son,
Will be an unforgettable ride.

Many folks will cry and some will die and years from that day
You would have opened all of America's eyes.
Rise, rise and let yourself be free from
The bondage in chains of how life used to be,
For those who came before me.
Now look at me being all that I can be
Because now you're dealing with true diversity,
With the Army, Navy, Air Forces, Marines,
National Guard, and me.

Standing hand and hand with every ethnic group,
Making the ultimate sacrifice for the boys and girls
Who got dressed but didn't have the courage to fight,
And that's alright, as long as they keep the homeland tight.

Because together we will stand and defend this great land,
Forgetting not one fallen Soldier, who came and took the stand.
My country tis of thee, sweet land of liberty, of thee I see,
Because everywhere I go the enemy is staring back at me,
And I realize that "Freedom" just isn't free.

Funeral

When was the last time you went to a funeral?
As you sat in the pew in silence, your cup -runneth over, your
heart began to swell within the cave of your chest.
As the lump in your throat continues to grow to the point,
which you could no longer hold it in.
A sigh buried deep within you escapes your body,
Leaving you drained, as if you were,
Taking your last breath. You weep uncontrollably,
Freely as if you haven't cried in years.

As the realization of the time and place hits you in the face.
You slowly look around because it's more evident of God's,
grace and mercy, as you rustle in your seat.

The images of your lifestyle are weighing you down.
Who's to say when you will get "that" knock on the door?
When the present time known as "here and now",
Will intertwine with the thereafter.
In a blink of an eye, your life will pass before you, like sand
running through an hourglass.

You silently pray as if it were your last living day.
Oh lord, I'm sorry. Please forgive me,
For not doing the things I should have done.
I know right from wrong and yet you still bless me,
Even though I'm not worthy.

Please tell me there's a place for me.
For I am a sinner, and every day,
I'm struggling to get free.
I'm addicted to the forbidden fruit
Of the tree (like Adam was to Eve),
And I can't hide from thee.

Some days I'm strong like David and weak like Solomon.
Please don't leave me. Help me to absorb the teaching,
You give daily so I can wash my garment.
Feed my soul and renew my spirit
So I can walk with thee and,
Others can see you in me Amen.

Happy Father's Day

Father's Day comes once a year and it is time to stand up and cheer. Thank our dads for a job well done for giving us an abundance of love, laughter, discipline, and fun. But most of all Dad, I thank you for being you, loving and educating your daughter and seeing me through tough times like only a father could do. I thank you for all that you have done, and all that you will do, because I am the luckiest girl to have a wonderful Dad like you!

Hardwork

Why must our hearts feel the pain of the
sound of the thundering rain?
When our mind is so confused—it's not how we love
Or who we love, for others to talk out loud—the love we
Share can't compare to any love
before—for it is the power of
Your love that takes me through the door—

Let them talk; let them stare;
I don't care—I love you endlessly
Our love will part any sea—don't let
Playa' haters ruin our thang—
Because deep down inside they admire our game!

Our heart does what it wants to—
I'm not sorry I feel this way
My feet are planted on solid ground, and I'm here to stay

Don't push me away—don't turn your back,
'Cause the vision of you and me,
Damn "G" it's all that—make me scream your name—

Make me yell it in vain, hit this love box right
And put out my internal flame—
While I'm giving up this—
Mad, Crazy, Wild, Freaky, Exotic sex—
The image so visualized, that it makes your mama wet—

I'm not a freak, but I'll be one for "YOU"—
Because when a woman falls in
Love with a man, it's hard to say what she won't do—
I will love you,
Honor you, obey you too, I'll be your
help mate until the end
—I will serve, you like a King because
your soul mate needs a best friend

There will be good times, hard times,
Bad times too—break up, makeup,
That makes us feel sad and blue—
Disappointment and discuss that makes us
Fuss—and some situations that make us lose a little trust

As time goes on you learn each other's ways—
And realize that it is hard work
Staying in love from day to day

Have I Told You Lately

Have I told you what you mean to me? You're the sun that warms my flesh, you're the vision that allows me to see.

Have I told you what you mean to me? You're my hope and inspiration that allows me to be free.

Have I told you what you mean to me? You're the air that I breathe; the reason I fall on both knees thanking God for the precious gift he gave to me.

24th Street

Thinking about yesterday made me smile, because growing
Up in the white house on 24th street in Nebraska made me
Wish I was still a child.
Boy don't I miss those days, when my only ambition in life
Was to go and play.

Oh, how we played in the street in
the summer heat when the
fire hydrant came on. Kids came
from all around and played,
without siren sounds. As the grown
folks reminisced on their
childhood and joined in on the fun.
What a beautiful day when
the neighborhood became one!

Ding, ding, ding, ding the ice cream man
is coming. No matter what you
were doing, kids went crazy at the sound of delight.
Screaming out of control at the illusion of getting some

cold treat, better known as summer gold.
As my feet hit the pavement on
the hot street, it didn't bother me, cause chasing the bomb
pop man for a block was the norm,
and it was worth it to me.
When the truck came to its resting place.
Kids gathered around, turning their
pockets upside down. Trying to
find a silver coin deep within. If you
pulled out a dollar then
everybody was your best friend.

The adults made their way down,
counting all the heads that
stood around. For this day was a
blessing indeed, because all the
kids sat and ate ice cream freely. With
smiles on their faces and
laughter in the air, we treasured that
peaceful moment without a care.

Hot Mix

My heart beats out of control at the sound of your name.
To hear your laughter, drives me insane
as I filter out the other sounds,
so I can hear you softly whisper my name.
Your touch soothes me and I'm lost in the honeydew
temptation and, sensation that moves
me, to allow my subconscious
mind to take a journey, to endure all the wonderful things
you have in store for me. Years ago I
was scared to get close to you,
as I laid in bed masturbating, at the
thought of the things you might do.
Feeling the heat from my box, wishing you would
kick the door in like a cop, pinning me up against the wall
with the handcuff on lock, I'm resisting arrest,
because I want you to be the bad cop.

Laying on the floor, I'm in heat
wanting you more and more,
begging you to tease, every part of me, insisting that you

take your time to please me. Shit, I can't
wait, I'm itching with anticipation
to feel your thick tongue stroke, me gently
on my love button. Pull it in nice and slow,
blow your hot sweet breath on that spot
so she peaks up, for the evening show because
I'm a superwoman and I need a little, little more.

Boy quite playing, I need you to snake the drain,
clean the pipe, dig in deep, like your drilling a well.
I need you to hit this fine ass like a
brother just got out of jail.

Now take a pause for the cause,
because it's gonna get sticky and icky as I toss,
your salad, kissing and sucking your ball "teabag style".
Sliding the index in just to drive you wild.
I'm a real woman and I know how to keep it up right,
putting a little wiggle, in my hips
just to let you know I will play with the tip.
Baby, how does it feel for this tight,
juicy pulsating box to make the shaft
disappear, deep, deep in the mix.

Poppy, it's slippery when it's wet,
so you might want to get a better grip.

I got your toes curled up, and now
you've picked up the pace
like you're in a 100 –Meter race.
I love it that you are a "Tony the Tiger" fan
when you yell out this, joy box is great.
If you're feeling freaky today, we can go to
Broke Back Mountain and let the
hot wax, fall where it may,
because there's nothing wrong when grown folks
whisper, the lyrical lyrics of "Let's get it on."

How Do I?

How do I not worry about tomorrow
when today is weighing me down?
How do I keep my faith when it feels as if He's not around?
How do I find the strength to go on,
when I'm mentally drained,
Physically weak, because my body does not
absorb the nutrients from the food I eat?
How do I move my feet from the quicksand?
How do I catch my breath when it feels like my last one?
How do you?
You quit trying and stretch your hand to thee,
and in the midst of your confusion,
Our father will set you free.

How Long

For years, we have been on the battlefield. Our garments are worn, our bodies are tired and our hearts are heavy. Yet we continue to labor for the possibility of one day being free from the injustice imparted upon us.

As I stand out on this limb, I hope for equality. But, how can this be, when today those who judge us are unable to comprehend the struggles of yesterday? A struggle that began in 1841 where women made the ultimate sacrifice, without being violent they gave up their lives for a beginning that has no end.

How long? I ask myself shall we suffer the burdens from those days. For those days are no longer a reflection of the past, as we come face to face in the 21st-century workplace.

How long shall our hearts feel the pain of injustice and prejudiced images that stain the membrane of our ancestors, as we filter through life wishing, and still waiting for true equality for all women?

As I stand and observe my surroundings, it gives me the impression of being balanced. As I take my

blinders off, reality sets in and I shake my head
and say, "Things have not changed much from our
mother's days. For her days were filled with heartache
and pain. After 169 years, we women of this great
nation are still fighting for the same things."

The pioneers of yesterday are gone. They paved the way
and gave us a glimpse of the light for us to carry on. So, I
challenge all my sisters to take a stand and make a change
this day. Our actions are someone else's hopes and dreams,
the inspiration to a picture that has not yet been seen.

Who will be the first to start a new transformation to the
great constitution that will enable women of all nationalities
to gain their rightful place in this time, as history unfolds?
Who will take Sojourner Truth's place and stand and say,
"Ain't I A Woman", and "Yes I can?" Who will replace
Madeleine Albright, Blanche Scott, Anne Frank, Florence
E. Allen, Condoleezza Rice, Hattie McDaniel, Sandra Day
O'Connor, Shirley Chisholm, or LT. Col. Eileen Collins?
It is our time and we need not apologize for our strong
will and drive that keeps us alive. As we make our way,
trying to avoid tender toes that stand and block public
doors, they take our actions personally, to settle old scores.

Do not let their hard work from the days of Seneca
Falls, the suffering of women during the Civil

War, or the year 1920 be in vain. For I stand and
serve one Messiah, and Jesus is his name.

We are not a liability, but an asset to be adored. We are
the future, and we refuse to be ignored. As women of
this great nation, we are the fiber that keeps it strong,
as we confront those behind closed doors, asking
and demanding respectfully for a little bit more.

We fall down but we get up again. For a real soldier/
woman exhausts every means. Then starts all over again
knowing that my daughter's eyes are on me. From time
to time she has seen the salty water fall from these eyes.
These tears are not from shame, but of joy, knowing I am
willing to endure her ups and downs and uncertainties to
ease her burdens from the things others claim not to see.

There comes a time when every young girl needs to
see the warmth and serenity in her mother's eyes, and
when push comes to shove, also letting her know that
there is a fighter and a survivor that lives deep inside.

Out of the darkness came the consciousness of a
woman. Be proud of who you are and who you will
become. For you are resilient, strong, compassionate,
loving, and protective. You are a queen of queens and
courageous in all that you do. Because on your worst
day, it would still take two of them to equal you.

I'M Afraid

I can't lie, I'm afraid to die. It's the unknown
Feeling of having to wave this world bye, bye.
Will I know my time is near or will it happen
Like a thief in the night, and I'll be here no more?

Life is full of temptations that lead you in different
Directions. And I hope you don't turn your back and
Turn out the lights because I keep telling myself I need
A little more time to get it right.

I feel my time is slipping away. No one that I know has
Come back from judgment day (**but you**).
My subconscious mind is whipping me and the illegal
Smoke embraces me.

I can hear you clearly, but can't get free. I'll take one
More hit, then I'll quit then tomorrow I'll give you
All of me.

But tomorrow never comes and your foolish pride won
And now it is sad to say that this chapter is done.

.

I'M Not

I'm not a throw away, but an image of yesterday and a
Glimpse of what tomorrow could bring. So, I lift my voice
And sing, because I can still hear my heart beat that
Causes me to dream.
No, I wasn't born with a silver spoon or boots to match;
I was simply born with the possibility and I'm alright
With that.

I Want Desperately

I want desperately to wipe you from my memory.
But everywhere I go, something reminds me of you,
and I'm lost in the illusion of what used to be.

Love hurts and there is no shame in my game. I've spent
endless hours holding my pillow tight, leaving my salty
stains, wondering if my life was ever going to change.

I could blame you for all the wrong things that we've
been through, but everybody knows that it takes two.

Somewhere, we close our eyes and shut the
door, and the voice inside kept telling us
that love doesn't live here anymore.

It's a shame that we fell into that trap. Lack of
communication held us back. We lost our focus
and allowed Satan to slip in through the cracks.

Oh, how misery embraces company when your mind
is confused and you're struggling to get free. I'm on
my knees and Lord I'm asking you to hear my plea,
because this storm has taken control of me. Oh, how

I fight throughout the night, trying to figure out
how to get my life back and keep my family tight.

Every temptation comes my way; impure thoughts
cause me to stray from the love I built yesterday. I know,
there's no need for you to come to my rescue, I turned
my back several times and said, "I don't need you."

Now I've fallen and I can't get up. Looking up at you I
feel ashamed, knowing that I'm going to need your love,
strength, and compassion to help soothe my pain.

I stretch my hand to thee, please comfort me, and
give me the courage and strength to stand steadfast,
and not run away from the things I cannot see.

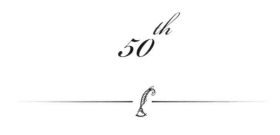

50th

I woke up this morning feeling blessed. On bended knees,
I confessed that I have done nothing so great for my
father to allow me to continue the air intake. I'm a half-
century old, divided within five decades, my story can
be told. At age ten, I'm sure I had a best friend. In my
twenties, I was breaking all the rules with illegal smoke
while trying to avoid suicide from not loving some dude.

Thirty rolled around and I seemed to find my way. With
a new career, a lover, and friend. Now my thinking has
changed, no more childish games, short and long term goals
is my master plan on which I stand and now are on display.
As I figure out how to increase my dividends, "The right
way". No more rent to pay, because taking on a mortgage
is responsibility with a Cadillac pushing out the driveway,
feeling blessed because, I'm grown. I'm in the chapel ready
to say "I Do" and it seems like I'm going to faint, thinking
to myself, this is my last date, but getting here, I will admit
has been great. In a blink of an eye I'm blessed with the
cries of a baby girl and a boy that I kiss good night, for

they are my greatest gift and they have changed my life
indeed, as I hear their soft tender voices call me mommy.

The big 4-0 started off right in Atlanta with the girls,
feeling sexy, ballin' out all night. Now I'm warrant
Officer bound, making history for 919A because the
first black female is now in town. The blessings keep
coming and house number two is divine. A conversation
with a co-worker went wrong and had me on Korean
Air one-way flight. I made the best of it because XX_
PRESSIONS became a household name, overnight
and I'm elated that I didn't protest to stay and fight.

Now I'm on the island where Luau and Nemo can be
seen daily; sitting back with ease, trying to figure out
how to get more cheese. Plotting and planning daily,
chasing dot three to pay me. Politicking to make a move,
recruited by the brigade and the DCO crew knowing that
Afghanistan was in my future real soon. It's an honor to
be going to WAR with the new Buffalo Soldier crew.

Shit, what did I do? Somebody smack me now, because
Afghanistan brought dark clouds. I couldn't see their faces
clearly, and the DCO had me sprung by his demeanor
and sermons portrayed often on Sunday, followed by
Kirk Franklin songs. Now the devil is at work and

the crew I once adored, I can no longer trust, for their actions betrayed me trying to cover their own dirt.

Time flies when you're having fun. My time has come to an end as I walk the stage for retirement, saying good bye to good friends. The forties was a rough road, but I proved to myself and those around me that I would not fold. God's grace and mercy has changed my life.

I thank you Father for changing my heart because Afghanistan had me parked, after dark with wicked thoughts. Oh how I thank you for stepping in and giving me a fresh start, steering my mind and filling that space in my heart when I had contemplated the end of 16 years with my husband, lover, and friend.

I'm fifty strong and I'm in the game. I sit in silence and pray because some of my childhood friends are in their final resting place. As this new chapter starts, I long for more patience and understanding to ignite my imagination, as I continue to write with passion, be bold, in each line a story will be told. On bended knees I will pray and let my father know that I'm feeling great and I'm eternally thankful for this beautiful day and all of its air intake.

I'M Sorry Lord

Lord, I'm sorry that I never took the time,
to thank you for the storms of life's lessons.
In the midst of your love, grace and mercy,
all I could feel was the pain,
Instead of the beauty of you lifting me up,
washing all of my stains.
I'm sorry for not putting you first in my life,
and it's funny in the midst of my fear,
and tears that when things went wrong,
I didn't call on my friends.
It was you, Father that I called night after night.
I'm sorry Father for speaking out of turn
when you took my earthly father and,
my mother's oldest son.
Once again, the sorrow and the pain consumed me,
and knowing the look on my,
mother's face will never be the same.
I knew nothing else to do, but to shout out in anger.
The sword that plugs deep into my chest
caused me to blast your name.

I'm sorry and I know like I've known
before that in our worst,
weakest moment, that Satan thrives on our pain,
using what he can to pull us farther away from you.
I'm sorry I was not strong enough to turn away,
but I'm strong enough now, to say that I love you,
and I need you every hour of every day,
If I'm going to make it on the uneven pavement,
that has been laid. You said that you
would comfort me. I will admit,
I wish the comfort, I was able to see would
ease my mind of its uncertainty.
I thank you for being a better friend
than I have been to anyone.
I thank you for not throwing in the
towel when I gave up on myself.
I thank you for allowing me another day
so I can once again see your power,
and glory in the wind, as it gently moves the leaves.
I will learn to be that tree and stand still so
my branches and leaves can move,
freely in the breeze.

Keep Your Hands On Me

Lord keep your hands on me, protect me from myself and the traps that others set for me. The forces of nature surround me as I stand in the middle trying to remain free and protect those precious gifts that look like me.

I'm scared as hell that I'm going to fail. I no longer want to walk with blinders on. Open my eyes so I can see all the images that are hidden in a distance that affect the real woman from rising within me, so that I'll be just as good or better as those who came before me.

The worldly things test me to no end, and I am often tempted and persuaded by lust and other things that cause me to sin, but I'm no fool because I know I only have one true friend.

My subconscious mind knows that the positive and negative are in a constant struggle over my soul. Please keep your hands on me and fill my disk with understanding that feeds me mentally and physically, and comforts me as I find the strength to tell the devil that he can't have me.

Love Hurts

Every day is a holiday as long as your love is here to stay—
Don't take our love away—I've been loving you for so long,
You can do no wrong in my eyes.

Even though I cry, I would not wave my baby bye, bye
We have come a long way—He doesn't beat me every day—
Only when I deserve it! Like when his food
Is not done on time—
Or if I interrupt a phone call, or
Ask him who he was with at the mall.
But he loves me, so?

It's been 3 years and no hospital bed—
the last time he beat me
I was almost dead—He doesn't get that mad anymore—
I don't talk back;
I just bow and give him the floor

I can't walk away—I have a daughter and one on the way—
What am I to do?—the baby needs her daddy and I do, too
I know, I KNOW!—I can't keep singing this sad song—
It's all played out and now it's time for me to see if there is a
Strong woman living inside of me.

I will no longer be a prisoner in my own home—
I'm not a violent woman by any means,
but enough is enough,
To end this horrible dream—
I have lived for ten years this way—
Begging and pleading this fool to stay—for what? —
Why did I have him stay?
He has torn me down and left a hollow display

It's been 5 months, 23 days, 11 hours, and 23 seconds when
I traded my life for less than minimum wage—
I snapped, I couldn't take it anymore—his hands hit me,
I hit the floor, I came up yelling, telling
that joker to hit the door.

He came at me like a mad man possessed—
Kicking and stomping until
He was out of breath—
Lying in my own blood, not able to speak—
I found the strength and made it to my feet.

This isn't how it was supposed to be—I
just wanted someone to love me,
For me—with his hands wrapped around my
neck, my knee found his manhood,
And put him in check— reaching for
anything to get my hands on—
With both eyes busted my vision left me—

Gripping the cast iron skillet with one
hand—I swing it with ease,
Connecting with the ugly forces that attacked
me—1 swing, 2 swings, 3 swings,
4—his face is indescribable as they
take me through the door.

Hmm, I should have listened to my
mama on that cold snowy day—
When she said, "Baby he's no good,
he's not right for you and you
Should get away" momma, I couldn't
hear her then—I was too busy,
Needing and wanting a man in my life—

I was looking for love in all the wrong
places and faces —instead of being,
Content with me, falling down on both
knees, asking God to send me a
Friend, a husband or soul mate, —who
knows if I had taken that route,
I might not have to hear "Lights Out."

Mama's Love

I never knew love like this before. Open my eyes, what a surprise inside of me. I can remember when I was a kid you see, no more than six to seven be. My mama placed me on her knee, with her arms wrapped around me so tight; at that moment, she was loving me with all her might. When our eyes finally met, it was the first time I had seen my mother weep. With a lump in her throat, she seemed out of breath as my little hands touched her face. I said, "Mama, why do you cry?

In a soft voice, unlike a voice I've never heard before, my mother whispered, "I love you more, than just words. I love you to the depth of my soul. I will love you endlessly until I'm old and see my reflection in the mirror as life's lines defines the time and my hair turns silver or dirty gold. I will love you when you're right and even when you're wrong. I will instill morals and values in you so you can always find your way back home."

"And when this wicked world turns its back, just remember, Mama will be there to help you pick up the slack. And when God calls me home, don't be sad. Try and understand that we are just visiting this great land."

"My life has been enriched and blessed indeed. My life has been fulfilled because God gave you to me. I might not have been the best mother. Just know, I did my best. I'm not afraid to leave this world and say goodbye for there is a new home waiting for me, yonder in the sky. Just put your faith in God, and let him do the rest."

Now that I'm a mother, I see things from a different perspective, beyond the highest tree. I never knew love like this before. Open my eyes, what a surprise inside of me. The overwhelming emotions hit me like a hot flash, as I gazed at the gift that God gave me. With tears rolling down my face, I embraced both kids and prayed to God that I have what it takes to be a good Mother, Wife, and even a friend; a strong woman that my family can depend on.

So, Mama, I'm sorry for all the heartaches and pain, especially the times that I made you feel ashamed. The times I didn't say, "Job well done," or sent you a birthday or mother day's card to show you, you're the one.

If I had to pick out of a million mothers, you would be the one. For the tough love, long talks and butt whipping, too. I'm a strong, aggressive, outgoing, positive woman because of you. I can't change, yesterday, so I'll live for today. And I, too will always love you endlessly until my dying days.

My Daughter Eyes

Looking into my daughter's eyes, seeing my reflection of me in her, causes my ducts to swell as the moisture flows freely. What a gift that God has given to me. Watching her in silence, she grows while I sleep. We stand face to face and I hope she's getting the best of me, as I expose my sensitivity by letting her know that there are many difficulties coming her way. Life is a challenge and we must pray every day that we can be better than today and make a difference in someone's life tomorrow.

Her eyes dance in the sunlight, dusk, dawn, and in the dark. I explain the importance of a mother and daughter's relationship. For at the age of twelve, she still lies upon my chest studying for a big test and I find peace and comfort as we talk freely after study time. In fear of this moment disappearing as she grows taller, because sweet sixteen is not so far away.

I wonder how I'm doing as a parent in her eyes. Her eyes are watching me, and as her mother, I stand and tell her that I want her to be a better woman than me. For this is my time to educate her without a break, talking about your first date, heart breaks, sleepovers, mistakes, staying out late, consciously praying that we will not have the conversation of her cycle being late. And if so, we'll cross that bridge and we will go. You see, it's my time to provide her with as much knowledge as her mind can absorb and store until a later time, as her maturity comes into play and she can always hit rewind on the words, I spoke of this day.

My daughter, I love you unconditionally and you are the reason I breathe. When the time comes that we don't see eye to eye, there will be those moments and I'm sure I will cry. Just know that in your toughest time, Mama will always, always be by your side. For a real mother, knows the internal cry.

A mother and daughter's relationship is full of hopes, dreams and full of honesty. No secrets or regrets, no communication disconnects, and definitely no disrespect. As you get older, you will always have both shoulders and arms to wrap you in, because I'm not just Mama, I'm your friend.

Standing In The Hall

Standing in the hallway, the average size of a fourth grader prior to the bell ringing. I look into the faces of the future generation, I ask the Lord to bless each student with the endurance to finish the race according to their own pace, for they know not all of the challenges that they will face.

As a teacher's, mentor's role model and more,
it is our responsibility to help them explore
the world as they see it with open doors.

Putting the emphasis on Education, playing sports (job well done) because a good education, leads to College Graduation that builds awesome relationships that causes you to think beyond your block and community and empower you to see endless possibilities of what you could be, as you rise beyond their expectation.

Don't be afraid to dream the impossible because
as your educator, we see Doctor, Lawyer, Professor
and a future President that stands before thee. As
we continue to plant the seed, giving you nature

sunlight, and water to quench your thirst as you
flourish on the big screen for the world to see.

Do not be consumed by fear, for fear is our biggest
enemy; but be engulfed by knowing that knowledge
is power and that you are intelligent, strong, and
resilient. If you believe it, then you can achieve it
as the body, soul, and mind work in unisons.

The time will soon come for you to rise and take the world
by surprise, as we stand and look at you with new eyes.

But until that day, know that failure is not an option,
for there is a village praying for the young minds of
today for tomorrow and to send them on their way.

The Curves

The curves of my hips hide the thickness of my lips buried deep between my thighs. Now change the look on your face, young lad, because the thought of smelling it has your nature on high. I'm licking my lips, biting my fingertips because I can't believe my eyes. Looking at this young delicious frame has got me saying my, my, my.

A warm sensation came over me, my juices seeped freely from the treasure box locked within me, as I imagine the thickness of your rod penetrating me slowly, and you expose me. Legs held high, you dig deeper and deeper in the tunnel that hides the sweetness that makes grown men cry.

I'm helplessly pinned on my back. The rhythmic motion brings on an asthma attack. As I feel the chills and thrills, I've never had it like that. I wipe my tears away as I yearn for the taste of your milky way, placing it on my lips, blowing softly, licking the soft spot behind the tip. Swinging my hips in a counter clockwise rotation, I can feel the pushing motion with slight hesitation as the aggression comes through shit, there's no telling what I might do.

Sucking it, out of control being your freak for the midnight show as I relax my muscle letting you know that "XX_PRESSIONS" can take a little more. You see, I'm a real woman and there's no shame in my game and for the record, baby boy, I'm here to do the damn thang.

So get your mind right cause it's going to be a hell of a night, you see. I need you to enjoy the pearl and make the magical swirls that make me work against the grain as your phalanges stimulate my nipple as I shout out "Can you freaking feel the rain?" As I start to gyrate out of control, creasing the back of the head while I'm freaking your tongue as if we were making our own private video.

Sighing out, sip all my champagne until I feel your tongue tickle my membrane. As my body twitches, with delight and the heat from the tunnel opens for the last flight and several good punches and it will be a good night but trust me, baby boy, I'll be ready for the bird flight.

The One I Didn't Keep

I feel faint. I'm sweating like five years of menopause hit me in the face. How do I say it out loud? I prayed for the red spot to cover the cloud and now I'm late. Standing in the kitchen face to face, I know that she knows by the scorned look in her face. In a harsh voice, I heard her say, what am I, what am I going to do? How could you be so stupid? Afraid to move as I stared into space. It's not about you, as I thought to myself, but I didn't have the strength or the courage to say out loud. As my frame swelled up from my tears not being exposed.

I can't believe what you're saying; is this a twisted dream? If so, let's turn the page. Because we are talking about a life, your future grandchild that you are encouraging me not to go the distance. Pretend that this isn't real, this is the only option that you (Mama) see is for me to throw away, abort, not to say a word and ignore, the gift that God gave to me.

I made a mistake and I will never be free from the nightmare of the crying baby that haunts me in my dreams. My voice, I have not found to boost it out loud, but I can hear the sounds fall softly upon my ears wishing you would go away. You confess you're a Godly woman, but you won't even take

48 hours to pray about this situation that will change the dynamic of a mother and daughter's relationship from this day. Because you're worried about what "THEY" might say, so you bully me, paint a picture that causes me difficulty and the best advice you can give me is to put the skeleton behind locked doors.

It's not all about you, I kept telling myself. I feel like I'm having a nervous breakdown, and the woman who gave birth to me is nowhere around. For I have seen you take care of other people's kids, time and time again, and now that your daughter's belly is full, your action is that of a stranger as you walk out with ease.

The unconditional love a child has for her mother is tearing at me and the moisture falling from my face effects my vision. It breaks my heart to know that in this lonely, scary moment, I don't have a mother, or a friend. With my sister by my side, holding my hand whispering I'm sorry and please don't cry. In a strong but soft voice, she said, "I think we should keep the bumble bee and God will make a way for all of us to feed." But Mama sitting in congress, vetoed that vote before, the words clearly left her throat. And the eyes of my first child, I will never see, for my action caused a reaction, and now I'm a slave to those memories. So, on bended knees, Lord please forgive me.

The Price For Freedom

There is a price for freedom in case you didn't know. There is a price for freedom because history tells us so. Every day we make a sacrifice to wear this uniform, but have you asked yourself the question, "Are you ready to pay the price?" like so many before us have given their life for justice, equality, and all human rights. So, you see, there is a price for freedom that represents you and me.

It started, January 15, 1929, when the proud parents held their baby boy for the first time. Thanking God for their bundle of joy, not knowing that he was the chosen one. The one who would endure more pain. As his parents, there would be restless nights that kept them on their knees asking God "Why?" As the salty tears rolled into fears, while others would contemplate the day his life would be erased.

Not knowing that one day people of all color would come to love and adore the baby boy that grew into a man. And as a nation, we would stand on our own mountain top and shout, "Dr. Martin Luther King."

April 4, 1968, was a tragedy. The world lost a phenomenal leader that gave people at that time a reason to believe in a concept that they could not see. Their actions caused a reaction, as stores burned to the ground. While others watched in dismay, knowing it was going to be a long time before things would change from that day.

Our people, as a whole, have made many sacrifices and accomplishments untold. Like, Adam Westfield, Elijah Bryant, Perry McKenny, William Riley, and James Walden during the Civil War. This won't make the front page because we would have to go back in time and look at the unjust treatment of how this world used to be. When dogs, chains, and water hoses were the pictures seen on TV.

Now take a journey with me, when times defined the line of cruelty and injustices that affected only black mankind. A time when mothers muffled the sound of a sick child, to avoid the heat of men riding on horses in white sheets. Crosses lit the James Town streets. A time when colored folks were afraid to speak for the fear of getting beat.

Even though I walk through the valley of death, I will fear no evil. I am made in the image of God with wool-like hair, and this is not a sequel.

So, my people, we are no longer living in the segregated days. This is the 21ˢᵗ century and all of God's children can, come together to play, and pray as we up lift the USA. United as one, looking at the multiple colors in the faces, represent the true diversity of this great nation.

One of the greatest men to ever live stood in a place where he could be seen. Because a vision with no voice is not a dream, but an illusion of how we want this world to be.

In order for us to have harmony, we as a people must fight without violence, so the world can see the balance of equality in mankind, as we leave the hatred and prejudice behind.

As we reminisce on yesterday, we stand with pride and wipe the tears away. As we sing the national anthem of the movement that brought us to this day, "We Shall Overcome One Day." On January 2009, America brought change with a new image, style, and grace and President Barrack Obama is his name. As we continue to overcome, "for I know in my heart, yes I do believe," that we, as a great nation will overcome.

The Storm

Life isn't about waiting for the storm
to pass you by, or asking why?
Life is about being ready and not being
surprised when the storm enters your life.
For we know not how long the storm will
last. With each storm, it brings a lesson.
As the wind blows and the raindrops fall
intermittently, it reminds us that **he's** near,
As the heavenly tears make music in our ears.
Without any storms, how will you overcome?
To know true humility and learn that all of
our blessings come from our father above
And not a man? We are not to ask why? But
to see beyond that moment and realize
That the umbrella will not always be by your side.

They Say I'M Ugly

They say I'm ugly and I won't fit in. They say I'm
stupid and they won't be my friend. At recess time, I
hear the kids laughing and playing their favorite games
as I stand alone, writing my name in the sand. They
don't know me and yet they call me names. They don't
know me and I bet we like some of the same things.

My day gets better and I know I will soon be free from
the other kids picking on me. A smile covers my face as
I see my mother and brother standing at the gate. My
mom asks me, "How was your day?" I turn my back
and wipe my tears away and then say, "It was ok."

There's times when I sit at my mother's feet and
I try not to cry, because I can see the hurt in her
face as she looks into my eyes. She said to me,
"My beautiful butterfly, why do you sigh?"

They call me ugly names and I don't understand
why. My mother lavishes me with soft kisses on my
forehead, as she caresses my little face and says to me,

you are smart and beautiful. For my child, you do not know the power that is cradled in your soul.

Life is hard, my loved one so, embrace each moment for what it is. Learn to draw strength from others putting you down while trying to feel good about themselves.

When your time comes, you will soar like an eagle without wings and recite words that make people cry, from the wisdom you broadcast that comes from deep inside. And it will be okay for them to call you ugly for you know now that you are Unique, Gorgeous, Lovely and most importantly, You.

Watching You

It was a beautiful day in September when I got the call that said hurry, come right away. Your father has taken ill with little words to say. Holding the phone in dismay as the buzzing sound came through the receiver bringing me back from outer space. My blood pressure elevated to its peak, I felt faint as my feet started to creep across the floor, holding the tears no more, wondering if I will get there in time, praying that God gives him a longer life line.

The ride from the airport was eerie. What normally takes 40 minutes seems to take days as I played back the number of times my dad and I had driven this route singing and playing silly games. Holding each other's hands, squeezing three times to say I love you through the silent grin, knowing that my dad was my best friend.

As the car reached its destination, I gazed out of the window staring at the front door expecting him to open it wide and greet me with his Billie Dee smile. The door opened slowly and a man's face appeared (not my father) and said, "He's been waiting for you". The house was cold and dark with a dim light coming from his bedroom. I entered the room with a big smile on my face, taking in my surroundings. I sigh and I wanted to cry knowing that we were not alone, for the angels were patiently waiting to take him home. I kiss him softly on his cheek, watching him sleep, wondering if I would get a chance to say all of the things, I was feeling inside. I gently squeezed his hand three times letting him know that I was there.

In a moment of silence, there was so much said when our eyes made contact. He grinned as I grinned back. He patted the side of the bed. As I sat by his side, he slowly reached up and wiped the moisture from my eyes. With his raspy voice getting weaker every second, he said, "Now, now there is no need for tears for you and I knew this day was near. I am tired, I am ready, and I have no regrets."

"Remember to live life and enjoy each moment, for time stands still for no one. Dare yourself to be great and know where all of your blessings flow from. Walk down the street as if you're standing on center stage knowing that you made it to see another day."

A chill comes over me while I'm holding his hand watching him sleep and I know it won't be long as I squeezed his hand three times, I whisper its ok for you to go home. I love you, dad!

Wedding Bells

It seems like I have waited a lifetime for you.
With all the temptation coming my way,
God whispered and said, "Stay humble and true."
I never thought in my wildest dreams he
would send me someone like you.

I can tell you my insecurity and fear as you
wipe away my tears. I pray to the stars above
I have what it takes for you to stay forever
and a day.

This is my promise to you from this day on.
I will be your humming bird in spring, as long as you
continue to be the strong rock on which I can lean.
I'll be a help mate until the end, being faithful to my
soul mate and best friend.

Life will be challenging from time to time, but I will
remain steadfast knowing that my Father put you by my
side. For that reason, I am filled with undesirable pride.

So I'll lift my voice and sing to the Savior we call the King.
Together, you and I will achieve phenomenal things.
I thank God for fulfilling my lifelong dream.

We Do Matter

Black lives matter and it's a tragedy that the world can't see that racism is still affecting this nation and generations of unborn seeds. "How long?" I ask myself must we cry. How long are we willing to stand aside and watch the opposition make a brash attempt of genocide in front of America's eyes? We as a people, black people, are to step aside and watch our brothers, fathers, mothers and sisters die in the cold, but yet, silent streets with weeping eyes.

Looking at those in blue who swore to protect and defend without hesitation or reservation of any man. They are quick to take the call, quick to react without probable cause. With no resistance and no threat, they are quick to arrest with no regrets. Their actions are praised for taking innocent lives and destroying families that sit in silence and pray.

In many situations our only crime was being black and being in the wrong place at the wrong time. It seems like "White Man Justice Black Man's Grief." My question to my people is, "How long are we

willing to stand in that line and watch the Jim
Crows of the past creep into the here and now?

We are trying to keep the peace. You don't want us
to erupt out of disgust, looking at the two headed
snake that we can't trust. Now a part of me (the flesh)
wants to say, if you want to fight then it's on. If you
take one of ours, we will take two of yours until we
even the score, with bloodshed at your front, back,
and side doors until you shout out, "No more."

Coming home from the cemetery in dismay because
the thought creeps into the frontal lobe that you will
not see your loved one anymore and it hurts like hell
and you want justice. It's your time to see, and to realize
that your great system you have embraced for years
has turned its back on thee. My question for you is,
"How does it feel to be a different shade of black?"

Now, that's not the type of person I am. I want to live freely
in a world and, or society that accepts me for me. Taking
the time to read the content in front of their eyes, and not
judge or portray me to be the person they want me to be.

I want to look to grand mama's promise land knowing
that our maker, our father above understands our
frustration as we wait for our consultation, we envision the

transformation of a new world. Where color is obsolete and history is rewritten without men wearing white sheets, no cotton fields, no water hoses, no whips or neck chains. A world of peace and harmony, where each man and woman can pursue their American Dream. A vision of a nation, our nation that opens its arms to welcome one another without a hidden agenda. Because when it's all said and done, we need one another to remain strong.

No black or white, no fist fights, and no weapons ringing at night. No white chalk outline nor protesting signs, saying, this isn't right. As a Nation, we have to understand that United, we can conquer all, but divided we shall fall, like the Walls of Jericho. My people, the time has come for us to stand up for what is right and not lose sight of the possibility for a better life for those coming behind us. Dare yourself to have the courage to do the work that others fail to do.

Where Were You?

———————————

Where were you when I needed you? I called for you
but you never came. Where were you when the stench
of the alcohol, sweat of a musty man climbed upon
my small frame, punching the life out of my tiny
womb while you slept two doors down the hall?

I'm older and it's hard for me to believe that you
couldn't hear him in the hall, nor the muffled sound of
my cries. And yet every morning you looked into my
brown eyes as if you knew something wasn't right.

I needed your protection, and where were you? Coming in
late, smelling like sweaty sex with faded perfume as if you
just climbed out of the bottle from last call. Working late
you say, but there still wasn't enough food on anyone's plate.

Where were you when I tried to get away when
he looked at me, licking his lips like he was a wild
animal on the prey? Where were you when he said
you're ripe and ready on my tenth birthday?

For days, weeks and months, I cried trying to find the right words to describe the torture from day to day in my young life. I wondered if there was a God and why he put me through it not once, but twice. Twice a month he pinned me down, daring me to make a sound as I drowned in my tears.

Even when you were at home, you were gone. On days that you didn't have to work, I held on to you like a baby kangaroo in the sack begging you not to go. As the crocodile tears rolled down my face, I looked into your eyes, hoping you would see me. I whispered to you, "Mister is different when you're gone and why does he always stay here when you're away from home?"

Mama you couldn't see me then and you can't see me now. My innocence was taken, ripped from me when I was just a child. Years ago I lied because I didn't want to hurt you, but damn! It seems like that's the only thing we know how to do.

Yes, I did try to commit suicide. Where were you when I swung freely while the rope that left a permanent mark on my tender skin at age twelve and left me lost and dismayed without words to say for seven hundred and thirty days?" The marks always on display and were a conversational piece daily, which caused me to run away.

I don't have relationships with men; to be truthful, I despise them to the point of genocide because of the one you loved and said was your friend. I am angry with you as I lay on the couch with my therapist and tell her how you failed me, your daughter, because you needed the love from some piece of a man.

I often wonder why you wake up out of your sleep screaming like a child, "Mama help me, he's hurting me." And now I'm frozen in this space watching you run in your sleep to get away from the demon that haunts your dreams. I can't help but think, "Is that the same demon that invades my rem pattern and causes me to be prisoner over and over again."

I see you and I love you. Mama I'm sorry, I know the rumors are true and that hurts me for someone hurting you in that way. Don't cry. It wasn't your fault and it wasn't my fault. We have to be brave to confront the things that kept us under their control. We will no longer live behind those bars with bleeding scars.

Today is a new day and we must live in the present and be willing to speak up and speak out, to possibly save someone like me. Mama I forgive you, now forgive yourself, so we can walk hand and hand as mother, daughter, and soon to be, friends.

Words Do Hurt

When I was a child I heard people say, "Sticks and stones may break your bones, but words will never hurt you." I beg to differ. I would rather have taken the whipping or beating, you could say because the sting from the belt would last for a moment, then fade away.

Your words, cut me like a knife and left permanent stains as a little girl. I tried to do what was right so, she wouldn't have to hear those ugly, nasty names night after night. I knew you were frustrated taking care of five kids, around the clock, non-stop without dad being there.

For years, dad was not doing what was right and both of your inabilities to communicate like adults brought on verbal and sometimes fist fights. The word divorce was the topic night after night and that sent him on his way. J&B with a little salt sprinkled on freshly rolled lemon, helped ease the pain. I was too young to understand everything, but I wish my dad would have taken me with him that day. Because for years, that scared little girl prayed that my grandmother would show my mother the love she longed for and perhaps that would have helped her internal wounds.

With tears rolling down my face, I looked into my mother's eyes with unconditional love like most kids do. Knowing that behind the words that she shouted with anger, was her pain and shame from her childhood days, wishing that her mother would have found kind words to say or display, warmth and affection that could be seen. Her actions and her negative words had her locked in jail, tarnishing the dream of a young African queen.

As I search myself, looking for the little girl to set free. I'm forty years old and my mother's words still hurt me. As her mother's (my grandmother) words haunted her for years, leaving battle scars, wishing she was an eagle that could fly beyond stars and find peace of mind as her Heavenly Father comforted her.

Looking into my daughter's eyes, I pray that I will be a better mother than her and my grandmother and that my daughter will be a better mother than I. In order to succeed, I have to be strong and stop the internal bleeding that causes me to reveal my insecurity and false pride.

When I find myself frustrated, I'm afraid of what I might say. The years of verbal abuse, unbecoming words flood my membrane, but I can't let those words escape from my lips. For words have the power that could affect the prospect of one's future in the male and female seed that God gave to me. As I cry like a five-year-old, I prayed to the Lord to make me mute and let me die, if I would ever speak unflattering words that could affect their drive while looking into their future eyes.

So the cycle stops here. No nasty or negative words, just cheers and praise of what I see. As I pray to my Father above, to cradle you both like baby doves, so that your wings lift you up from what used to be, as you look abroad knowing that you are loved and an inspiration to me.

Why?

As I look into this great big sky, I often ask the question, "Why?
Why am I here? Why have I been brought to a place with such
Destruction and pain? A place where innocent babies are
Hooked on cocaine and mothers sell themselves
To feed their high and ignore God's gift,
Which is a baby that cries.

Why do they allow themselves to fall into a pit without walls?
With nothing to grip and no solid ground to crawl. Where is your
Self-respect? Your pride not to fall by the wayside of life's trickery
Hidden in the dark. Don't be confused by the old rules, because
It's not you that was sold or brought.

Your ancestors paved the way so that you could have a better life
Today. Because you're close-minded and selfish as hell, you
Would rather give up, throw in the towel and rot in those folks
Jail. The illusion of your high has got you living in hell and afraid
To be the woman that you are, or could be.

Not realizing that your heritage goes beyond the bondage, chains
And scars, and masters getting a little chocolate bar. Do your
Homework and you will see, that the same people once locked
In chains were Kings and Queens of a land that was and is free.

So my brothers, where are you in the midst of all her misery?
Hiding from your responsibility, now isn't that a damn shame.
Its hard work for the woman, to do all the things that should
Be done, without a strong man to help pull her through.
Now, don't get twisted, women are the backbone of
Every nation. It's through us that produces creation.

Women have been the Kings and Queens of many households
indeed.
You can damn well bet that this wasn't their American dream.
They stayed there and didn't bail from their/your responsibilities.
While the man gallivanted the world without a care. Showing
up weeks, months, and years later as if he's always been there.

You wonder why the woman cries, her mood swings are high
and, her attitude at times is like I don't give a damn?
I reckon you would feel the same way if you felt restless and
stuck.

Now, King of free land, I know it's tough trying to be a man
and you have
Your cross to bear. Living with uncontrollable fear of a
Man in your life. Your father, your best bud to be, left and
destroyed not, just yours, but your mother and sister's dreams.

Stop this vicious cycle and learn to be a better man that takes
the blunt of

Pain with the rain so, that you will be around for Birthdays, Christmases
And every Father's Day.

Look to the sky and swallow your foolish pride, and realize that it takes a,
Real man to cry.
Be proud of your heritage to be Black, Negro, Buckwheat, African baby
Of the land, feared the most, has been through the most, and yet we still stand.
Keep your mind strong and don't allow it to fall into "Those Folks Hands".

We don't get the credit, but black folks built this nation.
Our ancestor's sweat, blood, and tears run through the heart and,
Veins of this land.
The power and strength come from a place that the average man,
Can't comprehend.

Our ancestors watched our mothers and sisters cry while masters took
What was between their thighs, while our big strong buck broke their
Backs in the fields at the whips that cracked.
They lived long, stayed strong, and had less then scraps to eat.
And it's funny for me to see, white folks eat pig feet.

My brothers and sisters, we have to be as strong as those who came
Before us. And realize that through adversity and pain, whips, dogs,
Chains, and water hoses that left a permanent stain on an ethnic group.
That was to have no brain. It produced, Abe Lincoln, Harriet Tubman,
Booker T. Washington, Claude McKay, W.E.B. DuBois, Fredrick Douglass, Sojourner Truth, Carter G. Woodson, Harriet Jacobs, Jessie Owens, Joe Louis, Tuskegee Airmen, Rosa Parks, Dr. Martin Luther King, Malcom X, Shirley Chisholm, Madam CJ Walker, Mae Jemison, and Toni Morrison.

The list of inspiring names goes on. You can bet, when
I hear the question why? This Strong, Positive, Outgoing woman,
No longer cries.

Zoie

Black girl's rock, revolutionary, non-stop, 24/7 around
the clock and it is evident that we won't be blocked.
With pioneers like Cicely Tyson, Maya Angelou, Oprah
Winfrey, Mary Bond, Gladys Knight, Whoopi Goldberg,
Phylicia Rashad and Keke Palmer, paving the way,
letting us know, that our struggles will pay off one day.

Not afraid to look back at yesterday, for it was those paths
less traveled that enticed us. The fear we felt within, move
us and our advisors telling us we can't, drove us to rise
beyond their expectation of wicked hearts and eyes. Even
when moisture rolls down my face, I fall to my knees and
pray, knowing I have the courage to survive another day.

So, I grant you permission with your malice intention,
to try and keep me powerless and in chains, because in
your delusional world, all black women have four baby
daddies, are using some type of illegal substance that
affects the cells in the membrane, are welfare bound, high
school drop outs looking for a handout. "So you say."

Now, please step aside and allow me to apply the colors to the canvas. Before I was conceived my father had already laid out my destiny with bright colors for the world to see. All I have to do is believe in me and keep my heavenly friend with me daily.

No matter how you try to tear me down, it wasted energy you displayed and you can't begin to understand or comprehend the power of the shield or pen. So I say to you, rest with ease, because we are growing the next generation that looks like me. They are strong and armed and ready to fight (not physically, because it's un-lady like) with words that are powerful as they write. Preparing to step into their destiny as one writes on her pillow at night, the next "Commander and Chief."

Thank You...

Printed in the United States
By Bookmasters